Replicate the Drawing

With a dedication to animal lovers

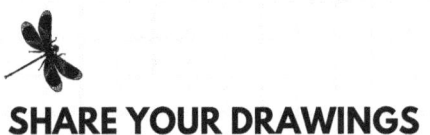

SHARE YOUR DRAWINGS

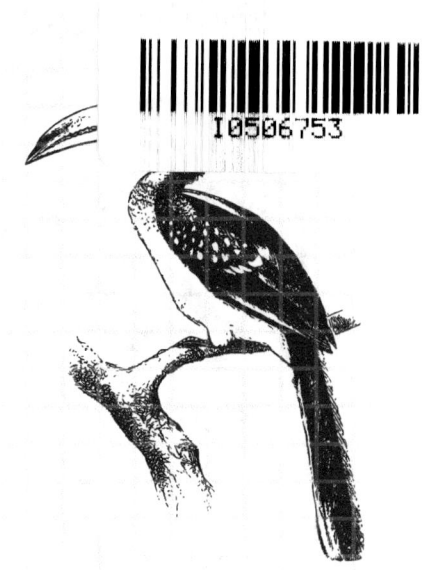

ADVANCED LEVEL

Galas Products

COPYRIGHT © 2020 BY GALAS DARIUSZALL RIGHTS RESERVED

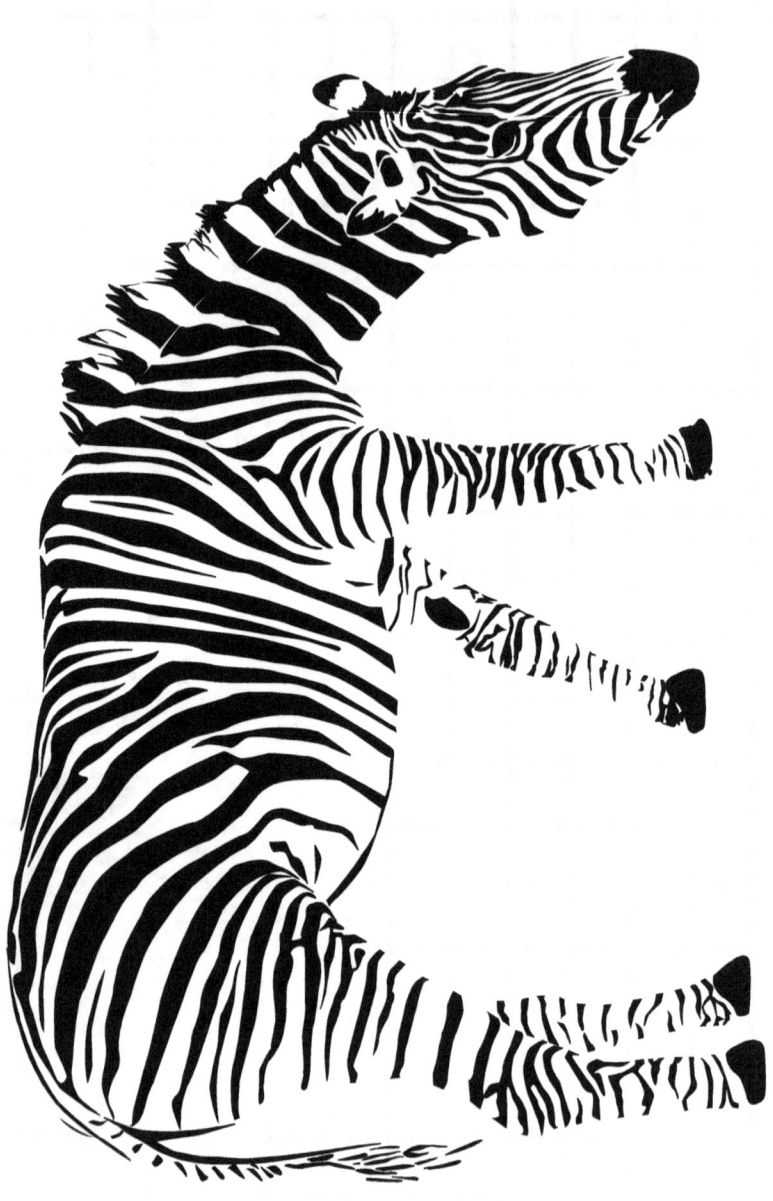

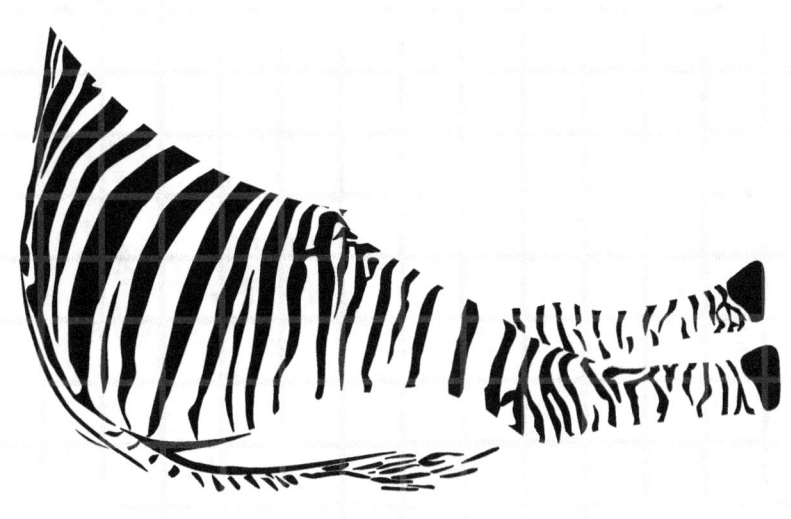

The zebra's ears show its mood.

Zebras are much more aggressive and much more dangerous than horses.

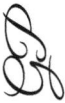

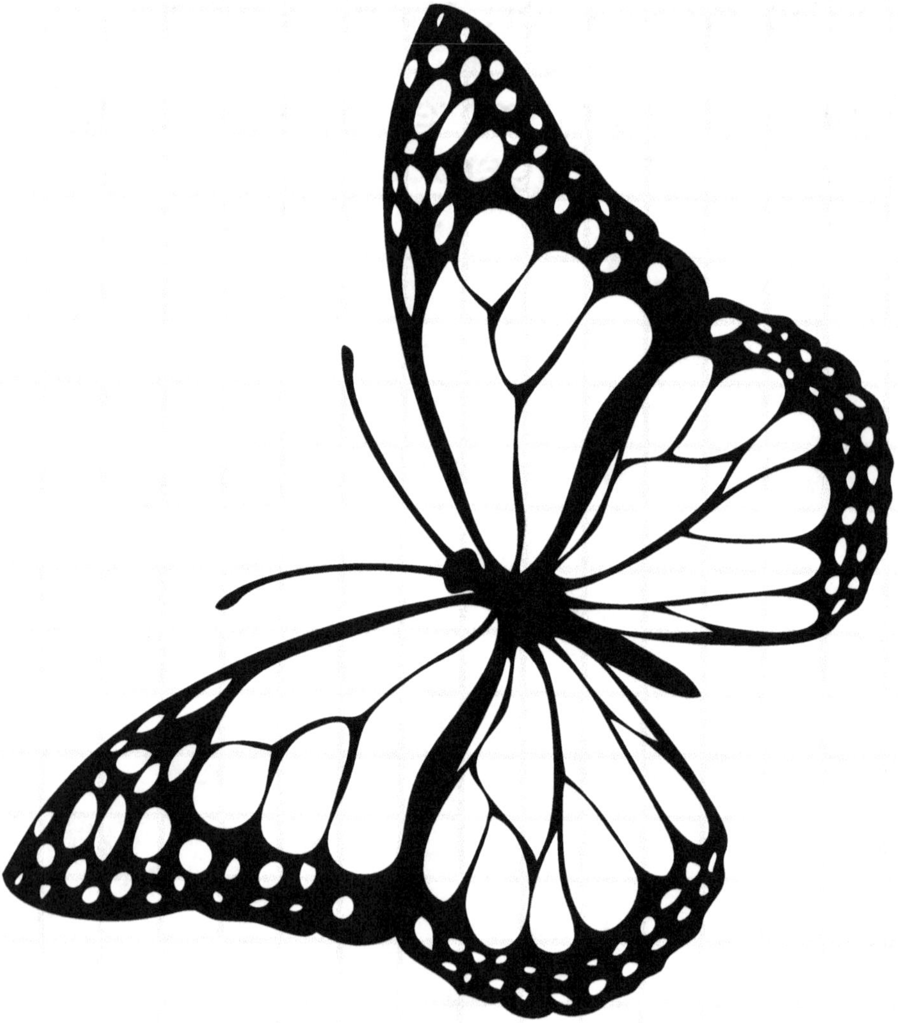

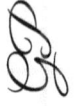

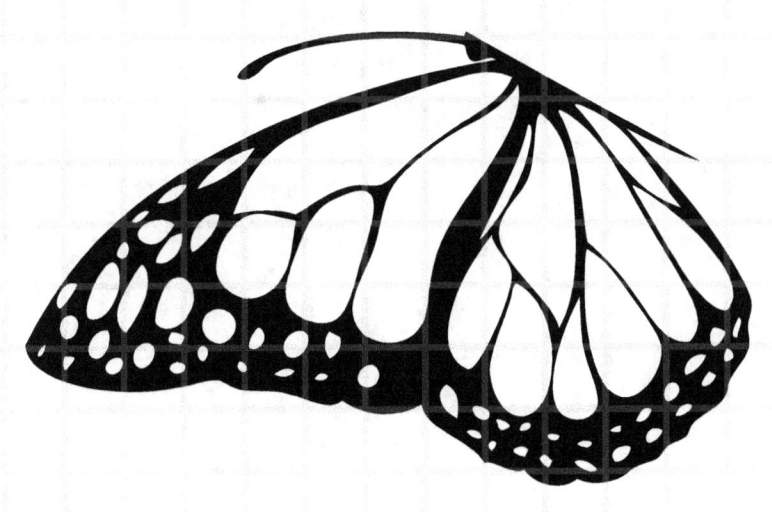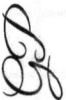

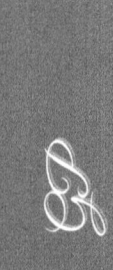

We distinguish over 150,000 species of butterflies

The life span of butterflies varies, depending on the species, from several hours to several months.

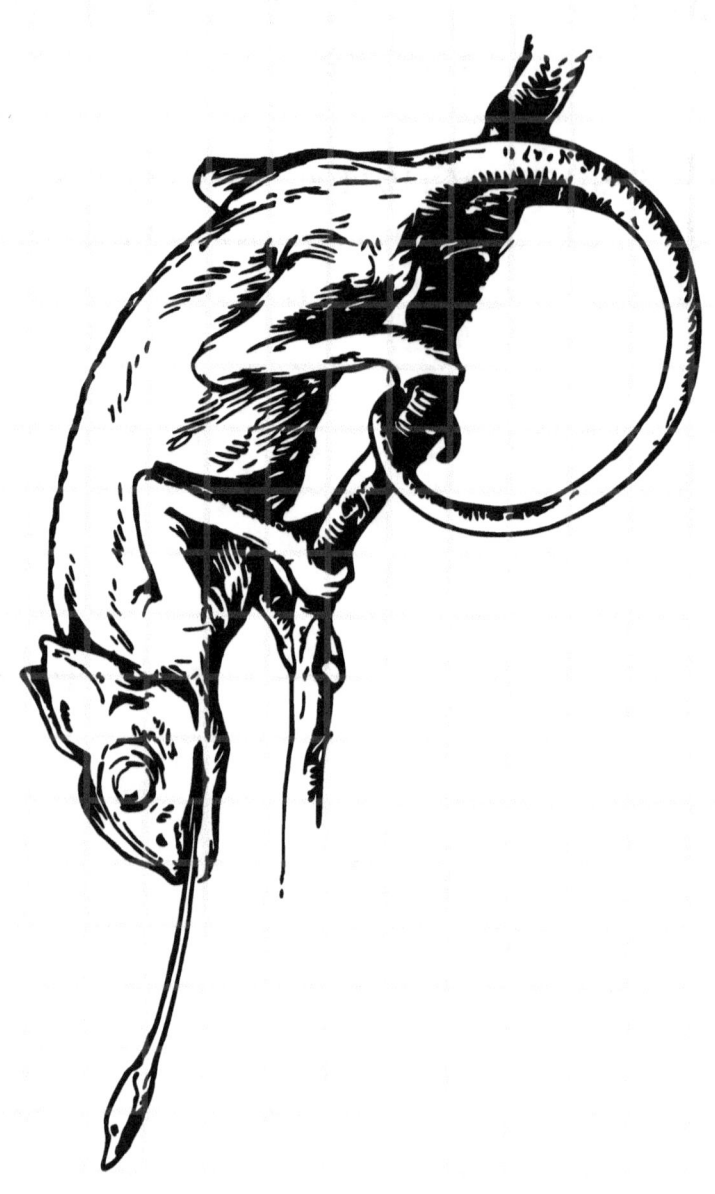

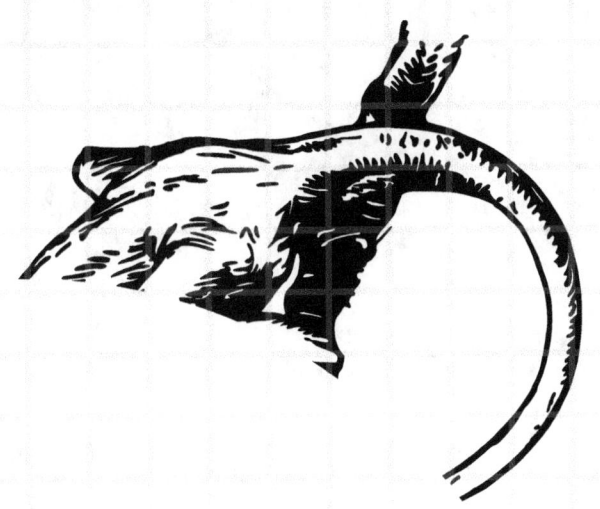

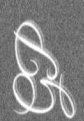

Chameleons are found in Africa and Madagascar.

They appeared on Earth over 100 million years ago.

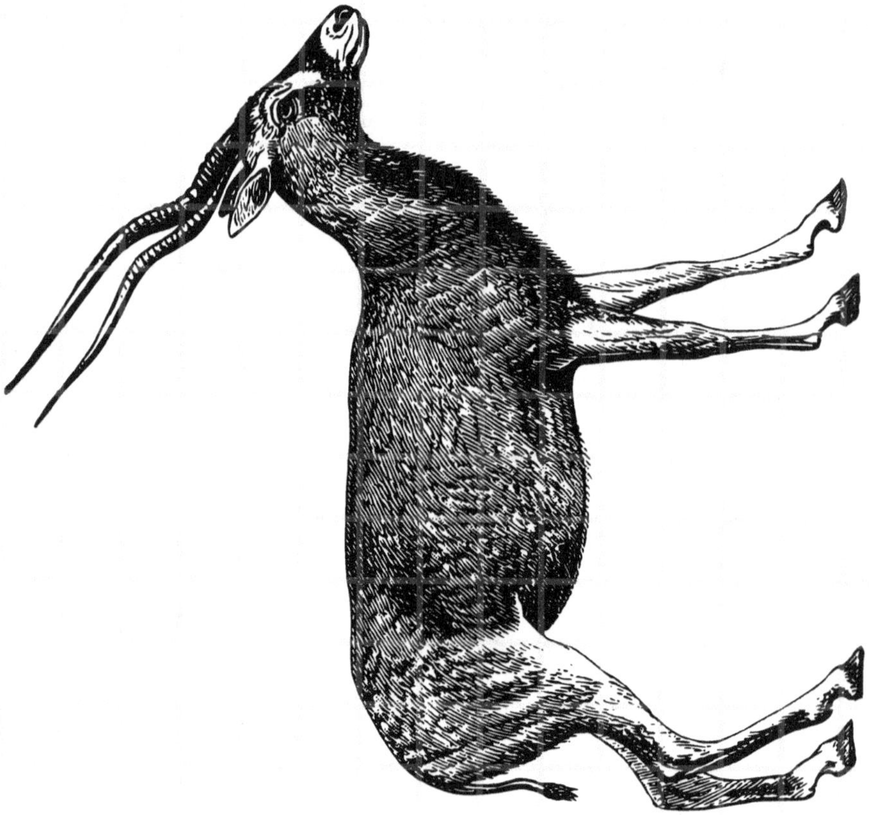

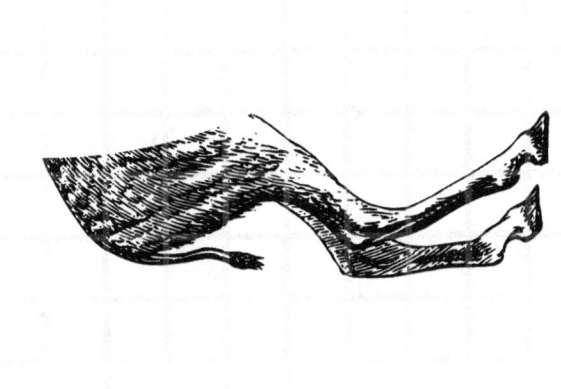

Antelopes live about 10 years in the wild and up to 20 years in captivity.

Almost all antelopes are social animals that live in herds.

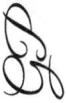

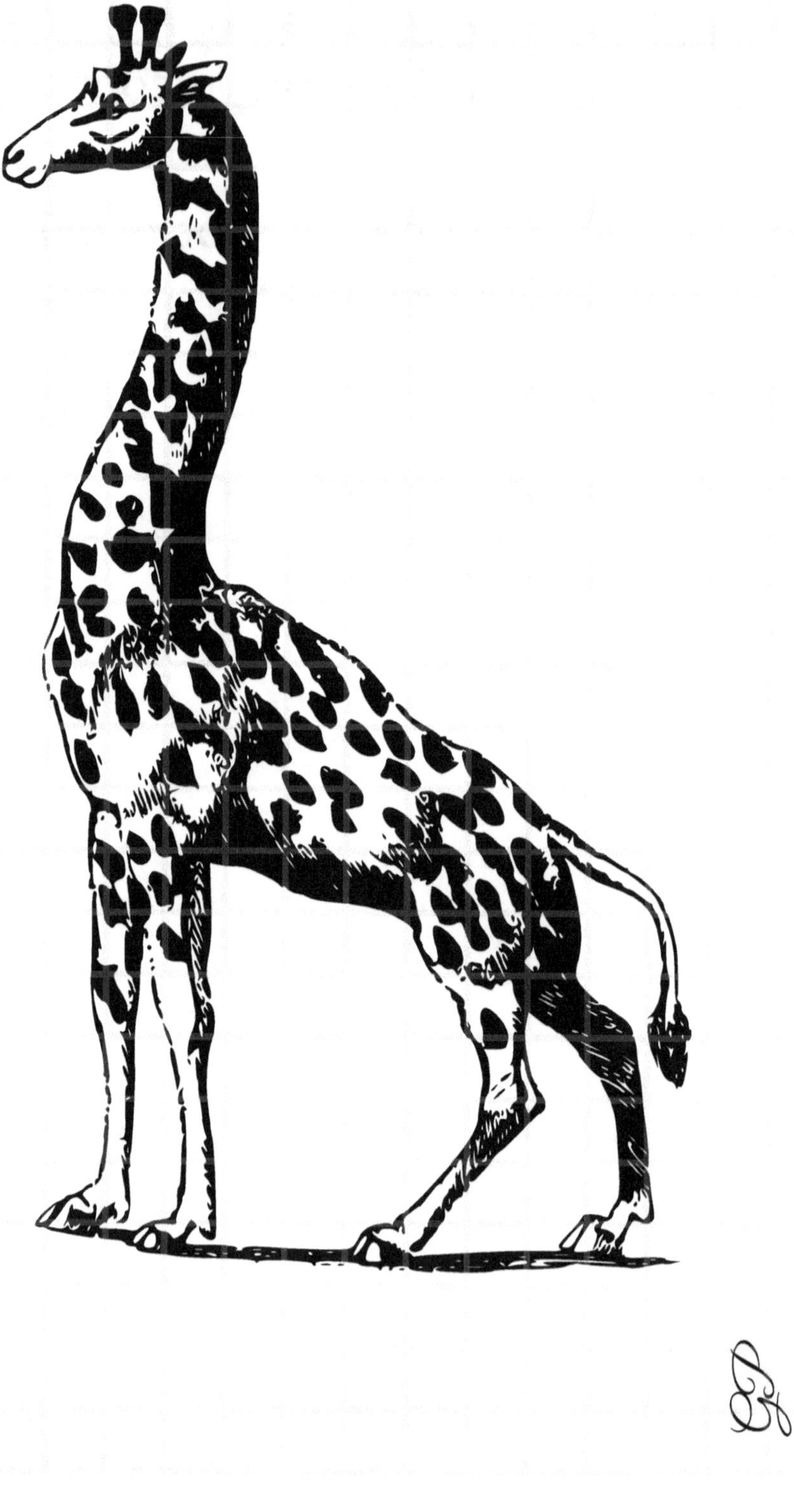

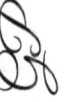

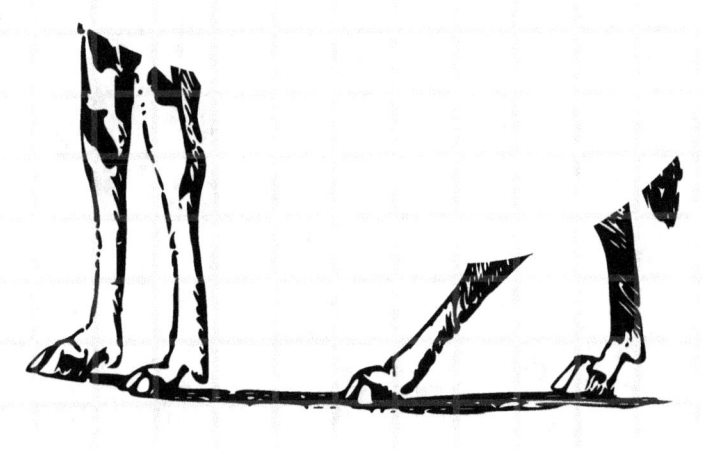

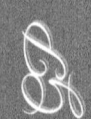

Giraffes eat more than 40 kilograms of food a day. .

Giraffes reach a height of 5-6 meters, males are taller and heavier than females.

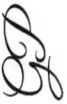

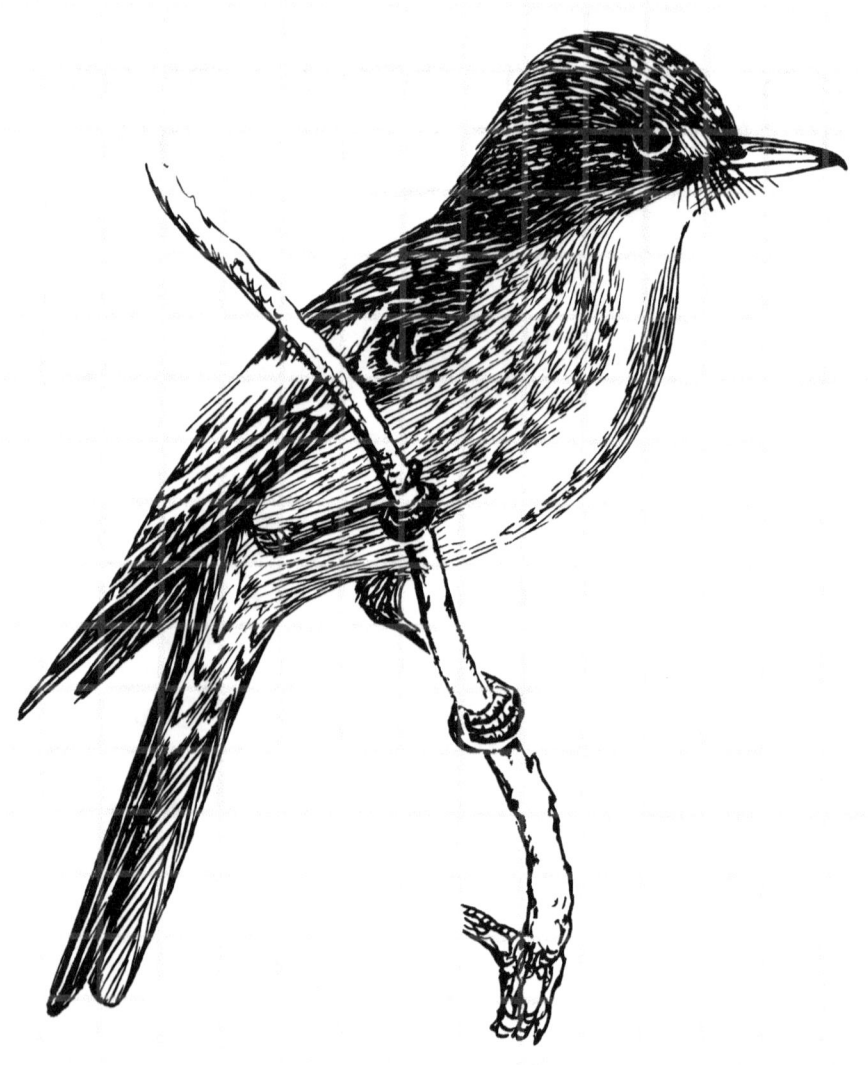

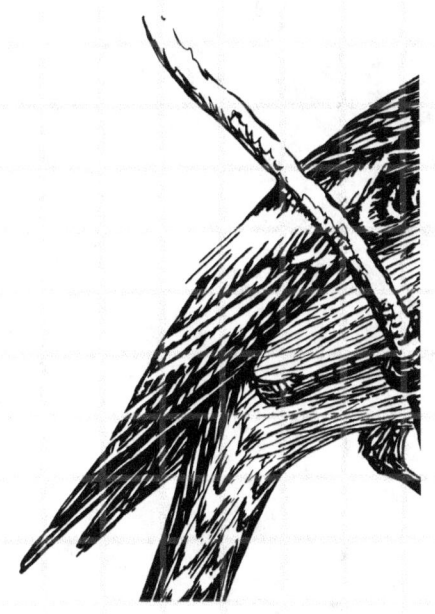

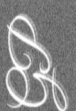

Birds are divided into 30 groups, 9,865 species, 1,227 of which are threatened with extinction.

All birds reproduce by laying eggs.

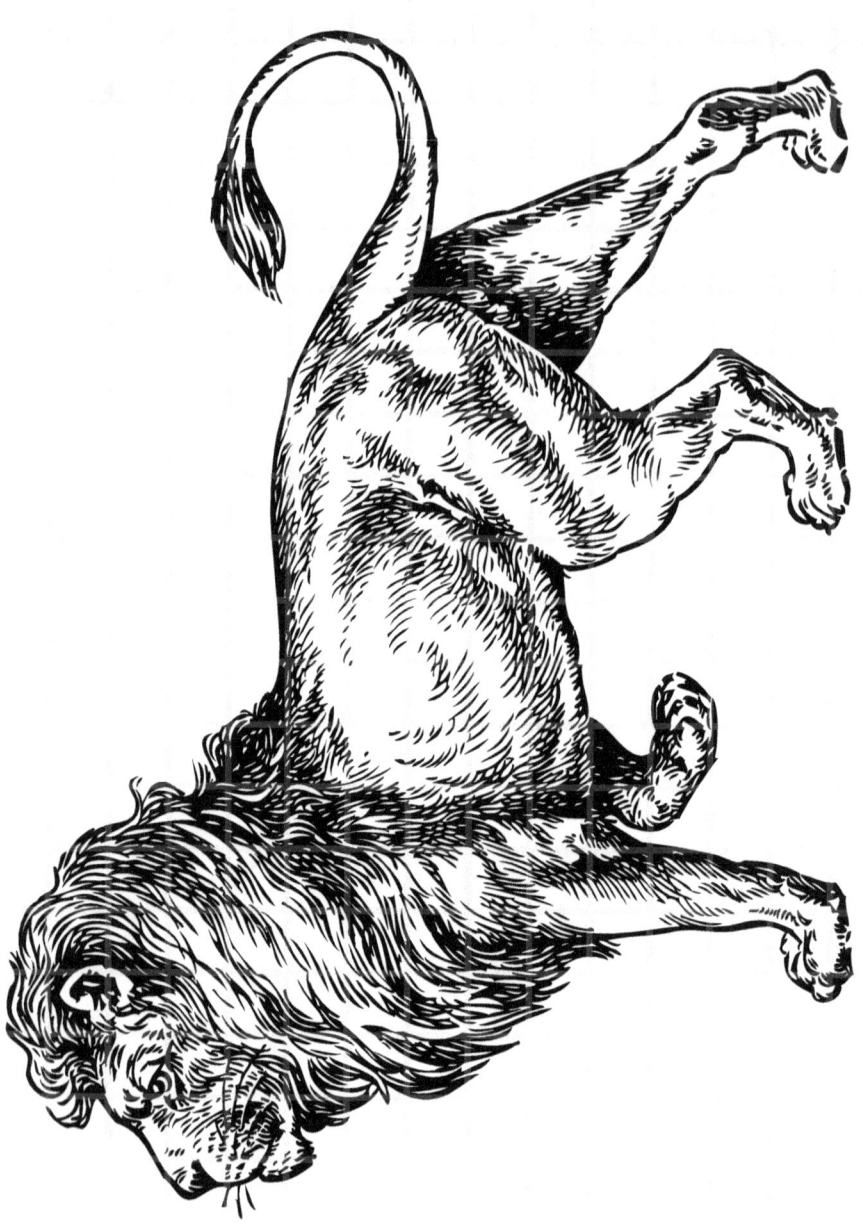

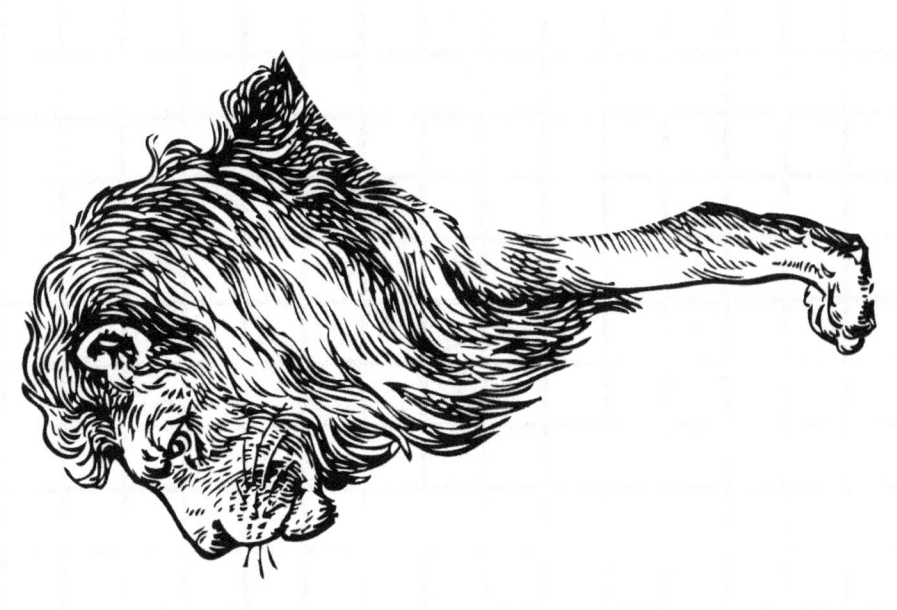

The roar of a lion can be heard from a distance of 6 kilometers

Lions, like humans, hug each other to build and sustain relationships.

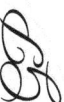

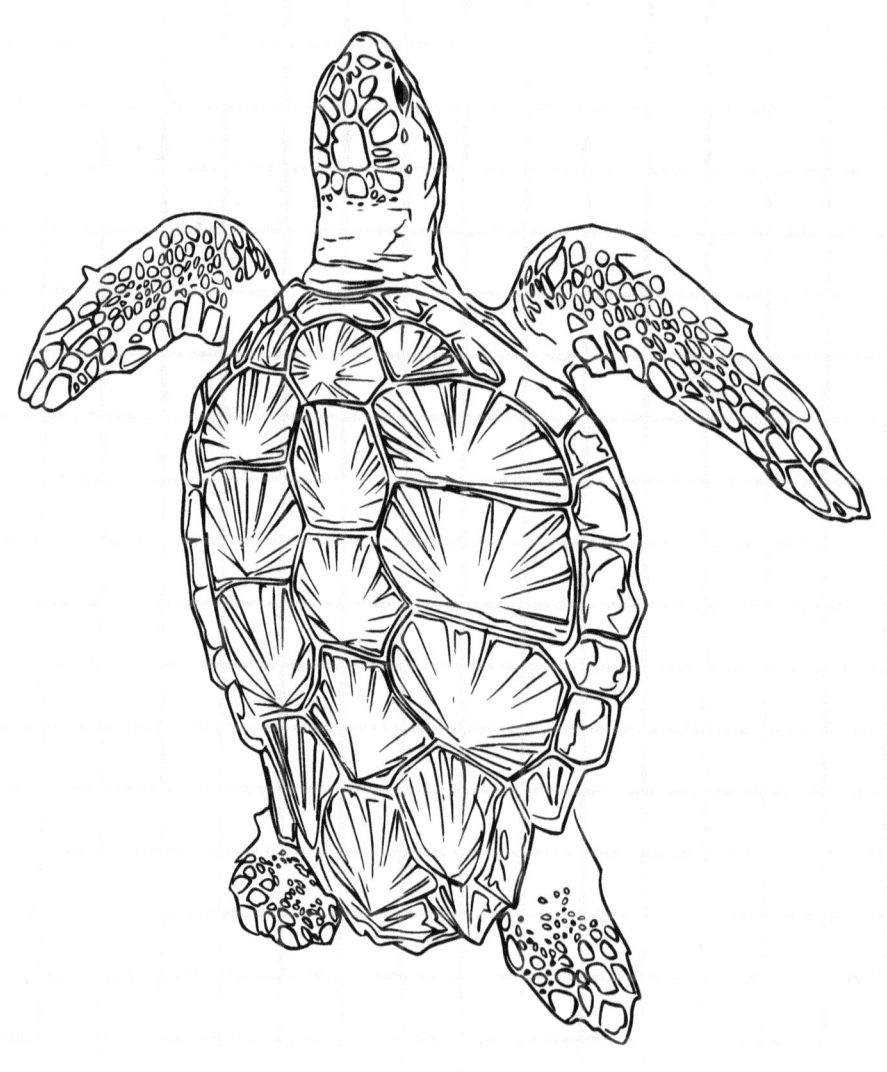

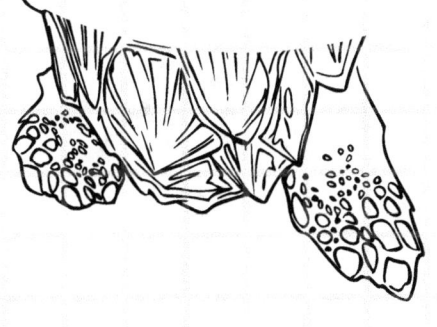

There are approximately 220 species of turtles.

The largest turtle is the leatherback sea turtle, measuring over 2 meters and weighing over 1000 kg.

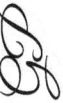

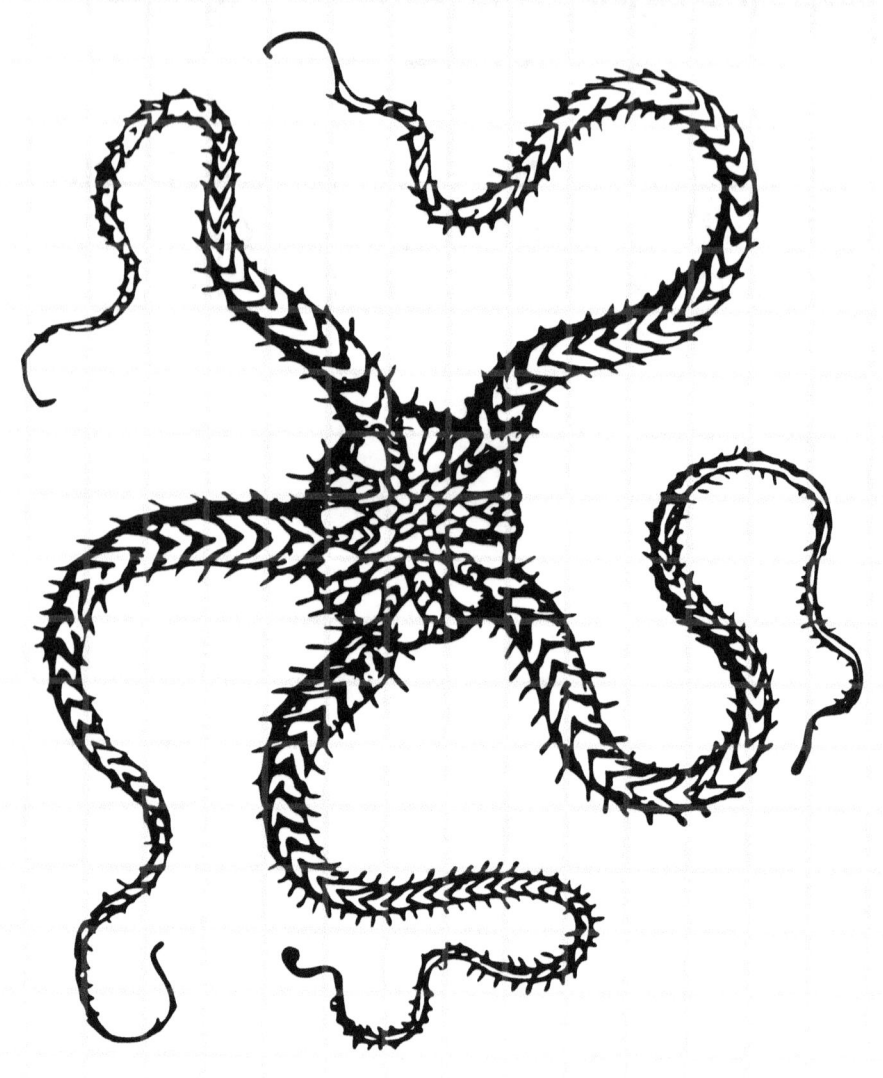

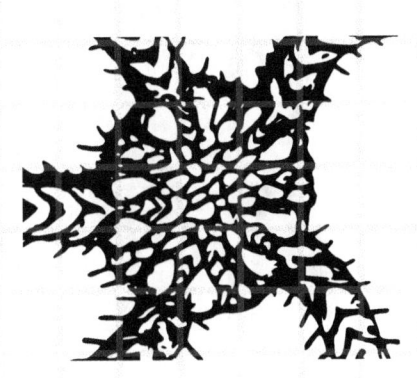

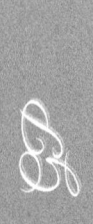

Octopuses have three hearts

Live octopus is eaten in Korea.

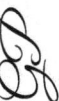

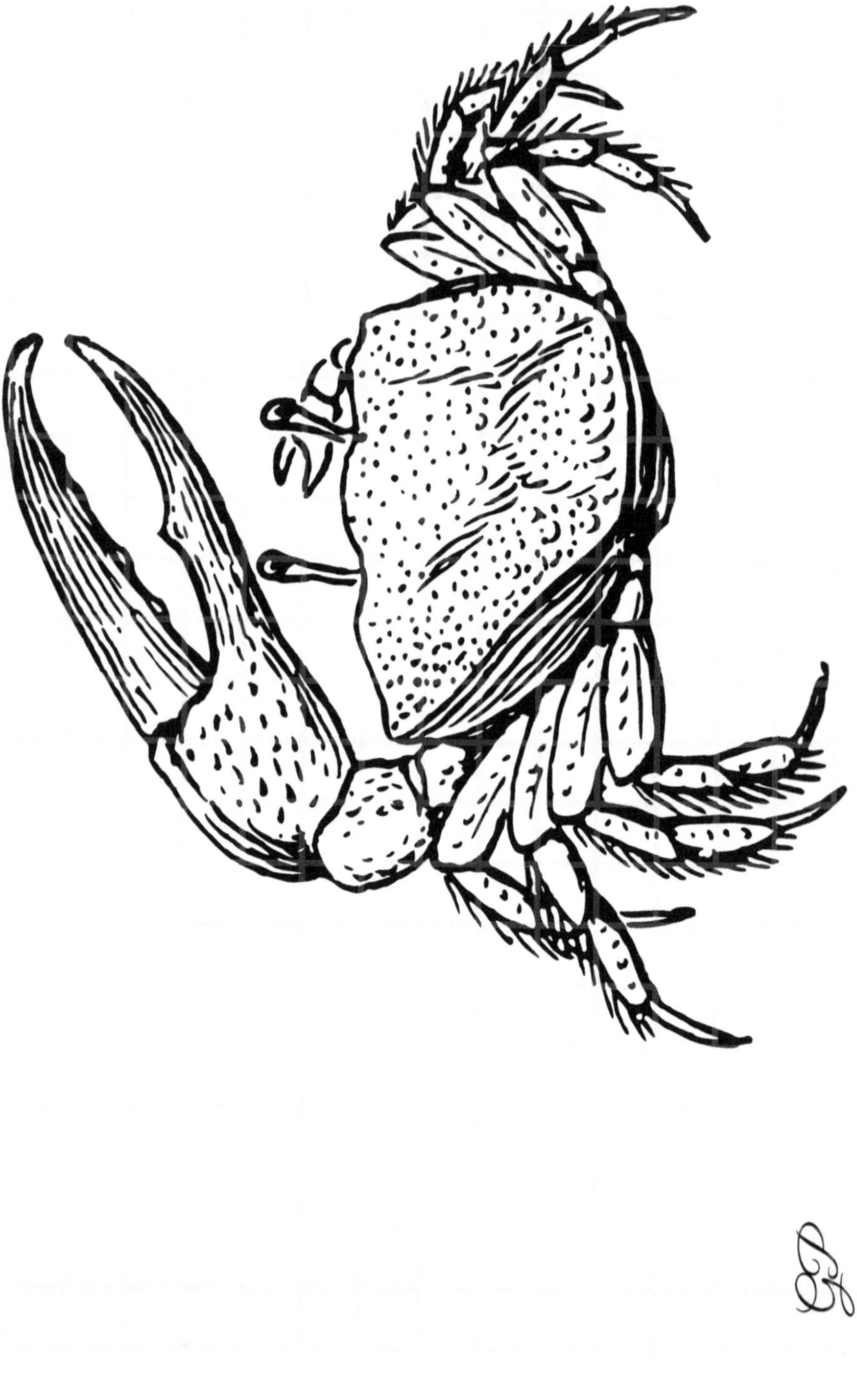

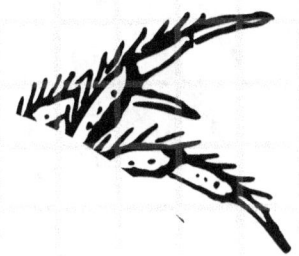
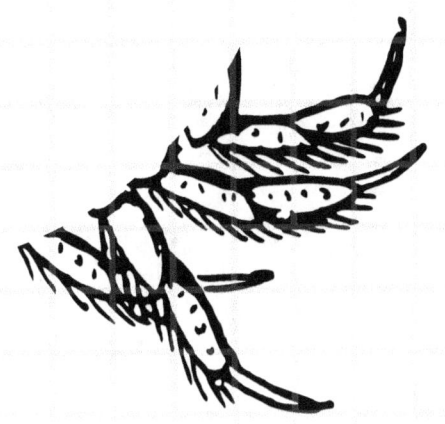

Crayfish are very aggressive and are omnivores.

The lifespan of the crayfish varies from 1 to 20 years, depending on the species.

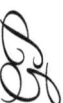

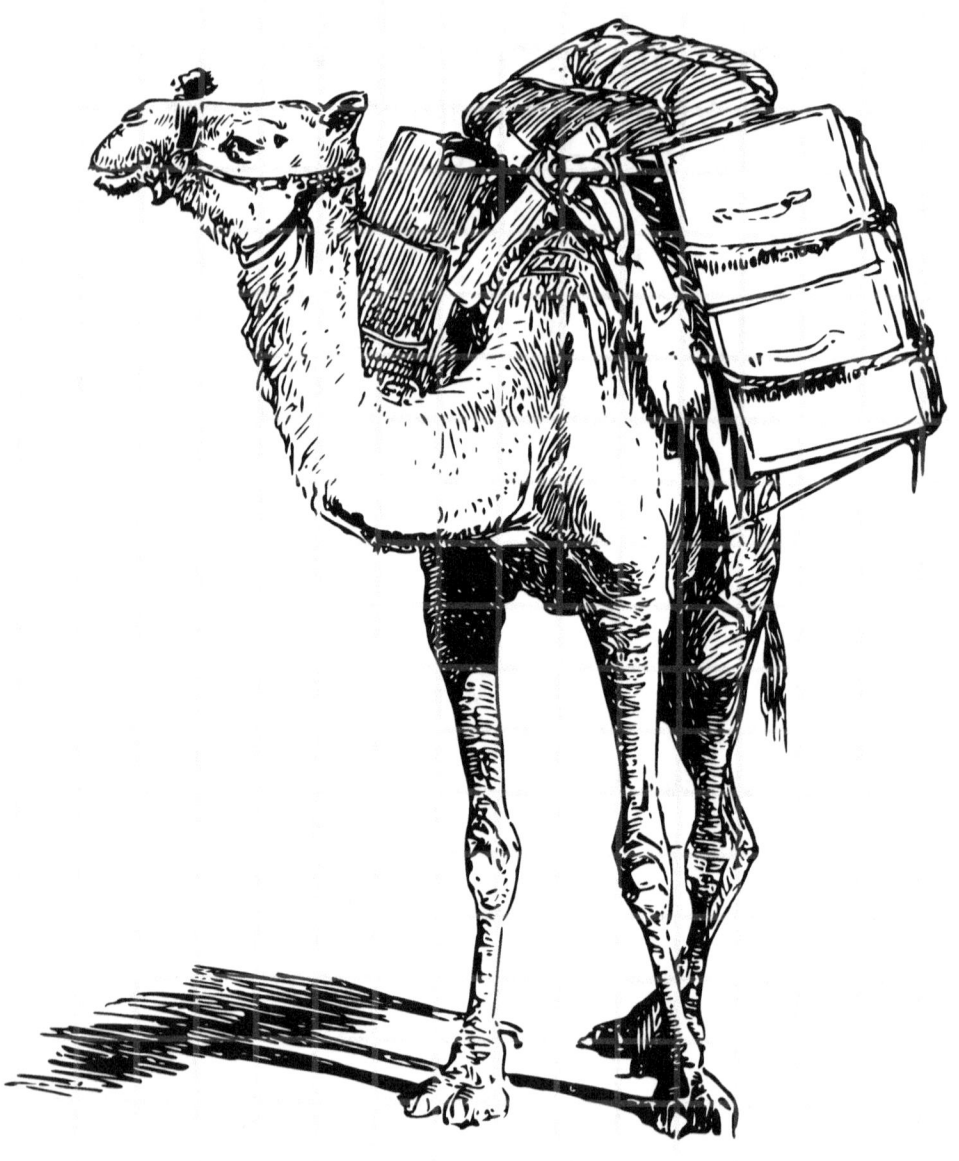

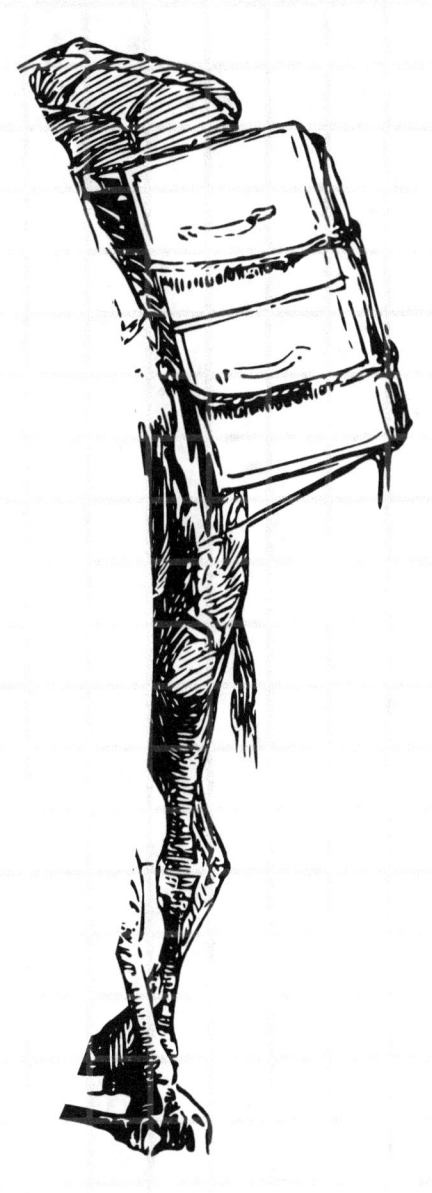

Camels have three eyelids.

An adult camel is able to drink 200 liters of water in three minutes.

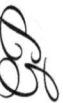

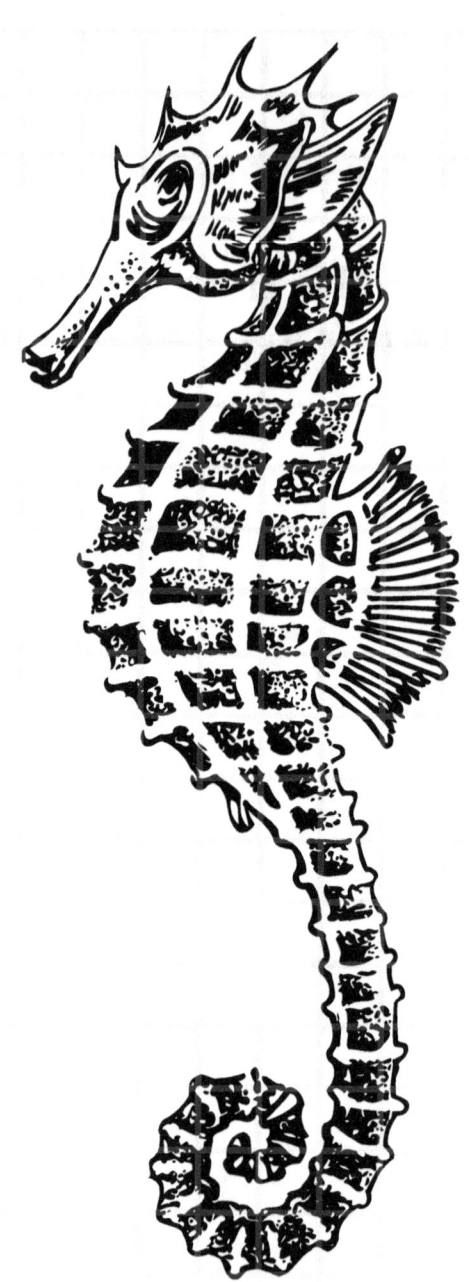

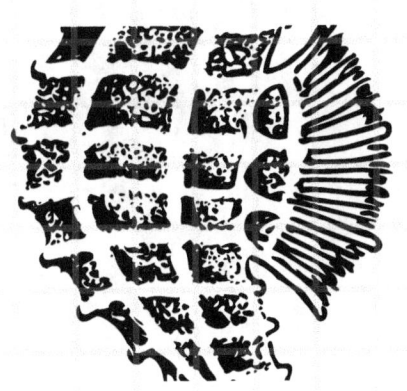

Seahorse It has only two fins:

It is most abundant in warm seas and oceans

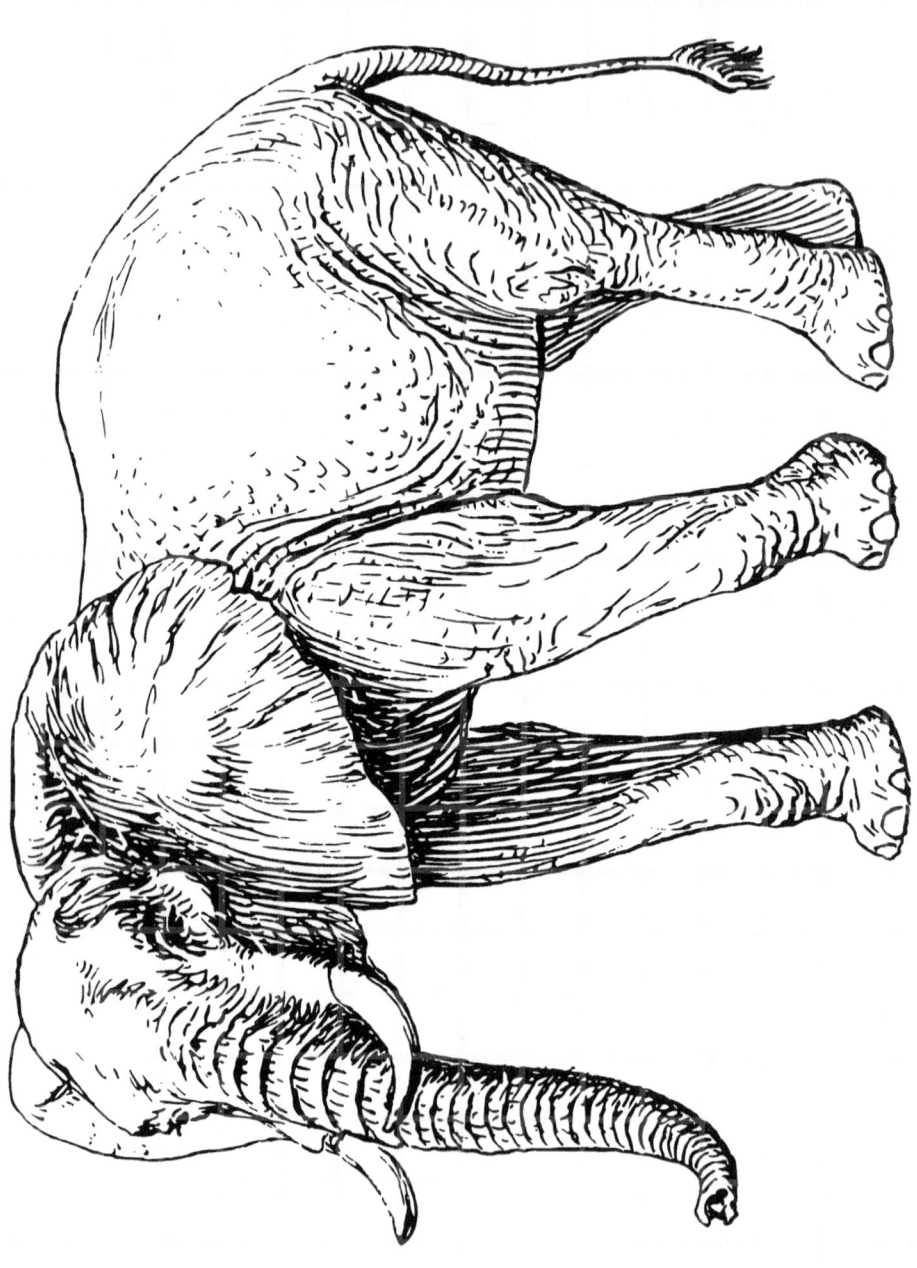

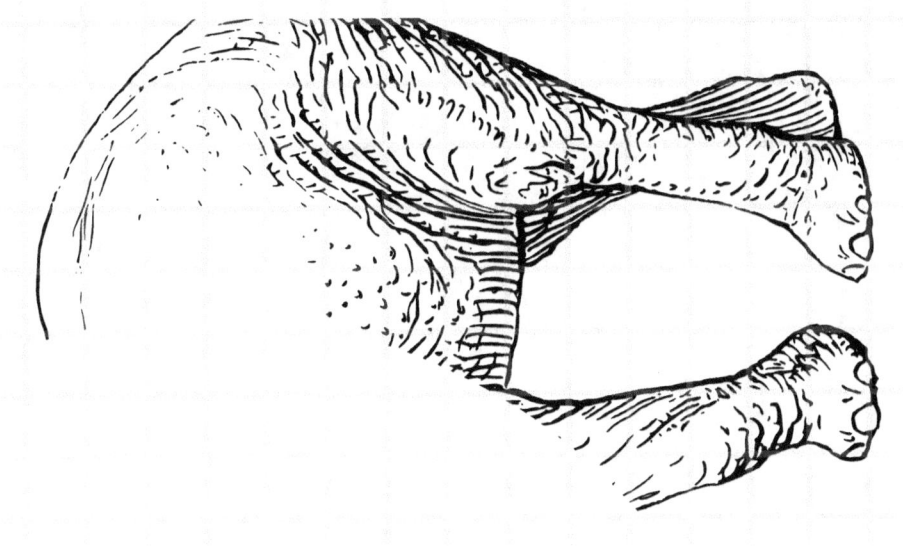
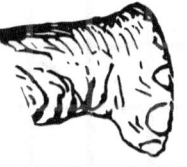

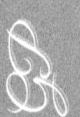

Little elephants suck their proboscis just like children suck their thumbs

The elephant age can reach 50-70 years

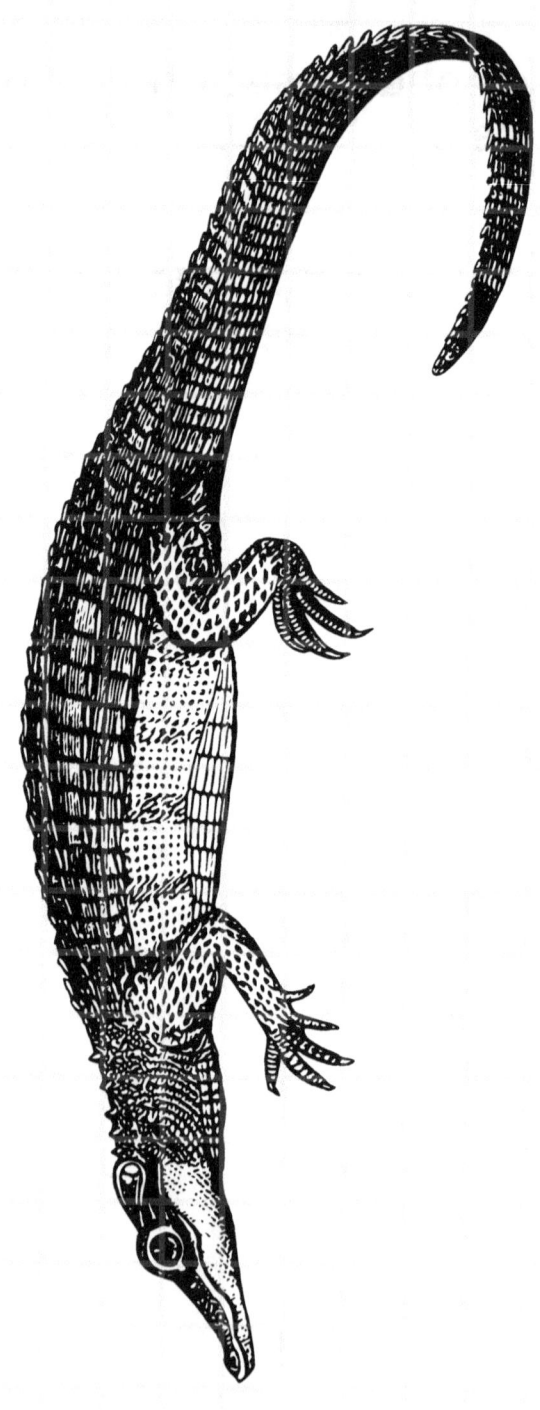

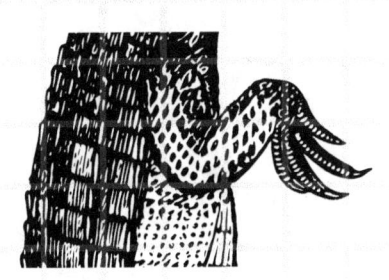

There are 23 different species of crocodiles

Saltwater crocodiles are the largest reptiles in the world

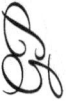

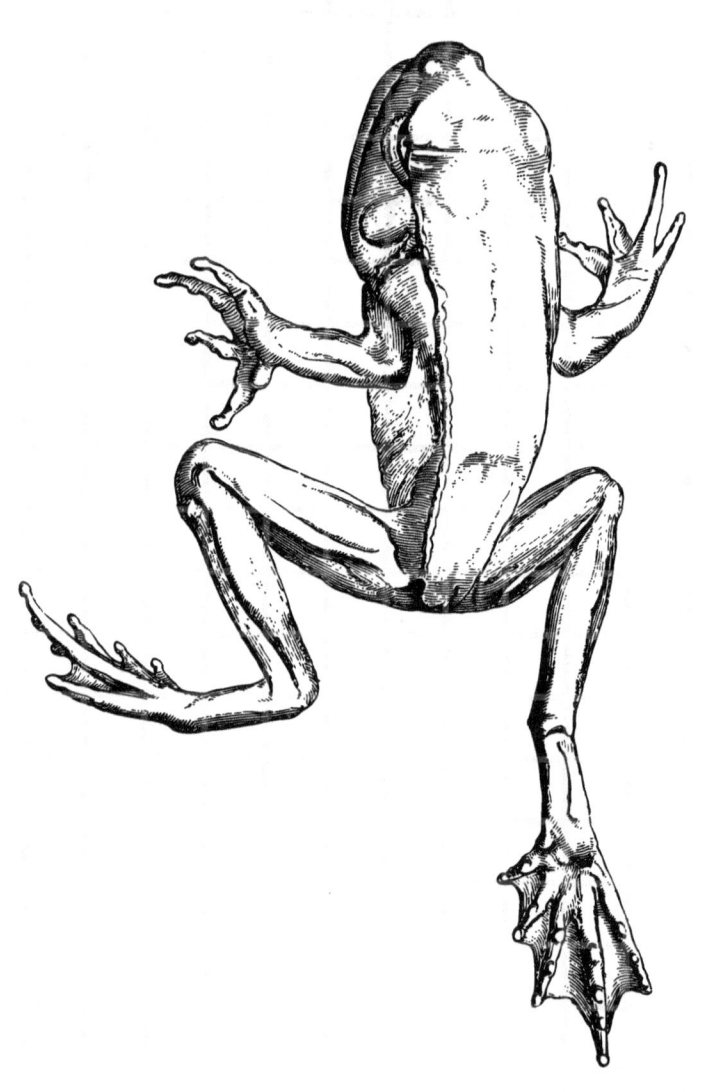

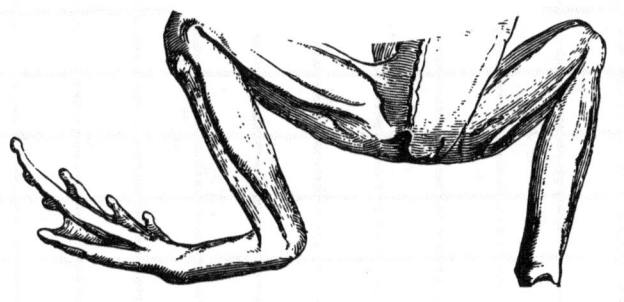

Not all frogs can jump, some have short legs.

Frogs soak water through their skin so they don't need to drink.

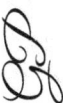

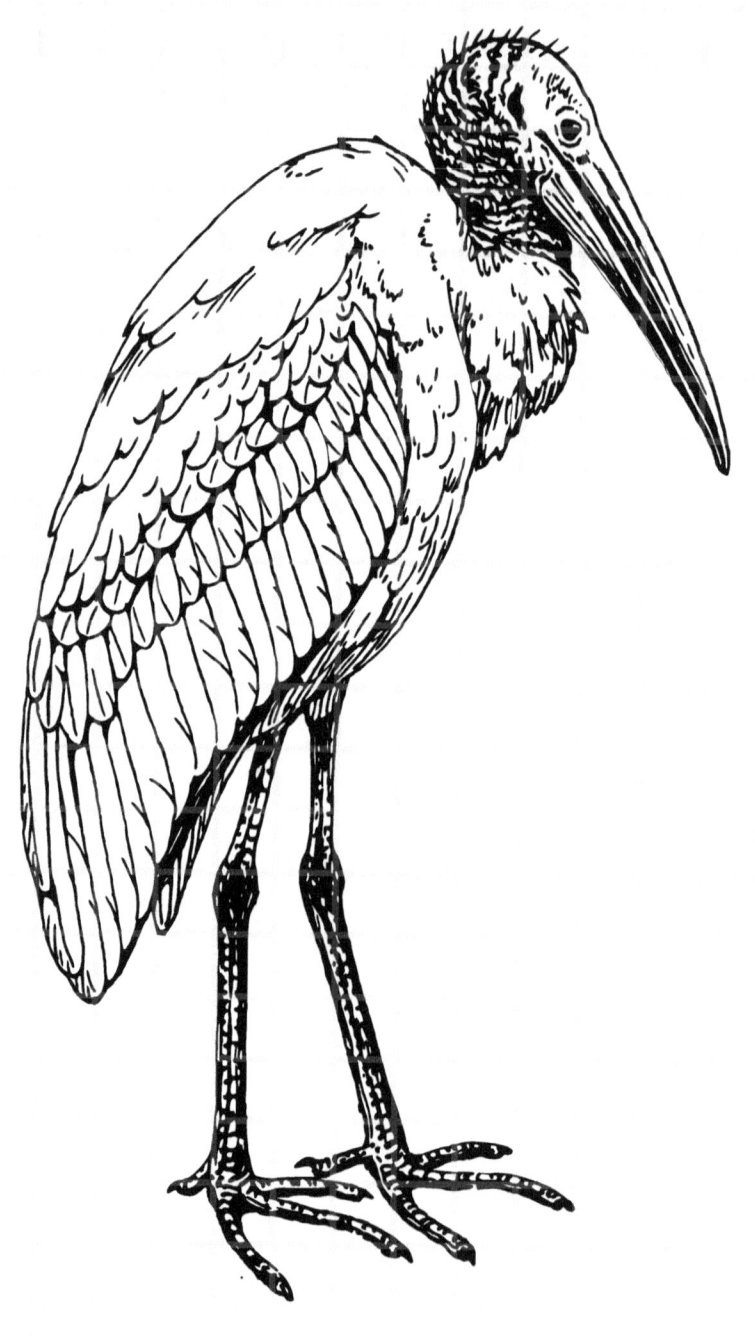

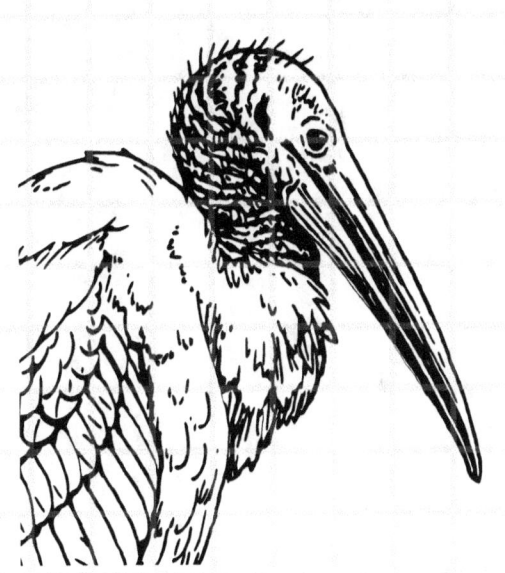

Ibises are omnivorous birds

Ibises are social animals that generally live in large colonies

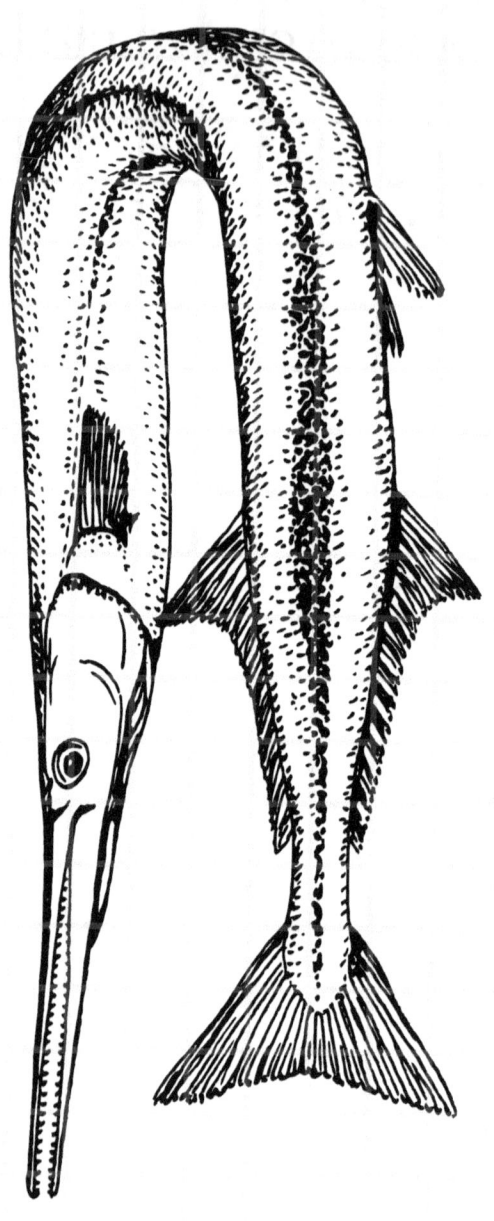

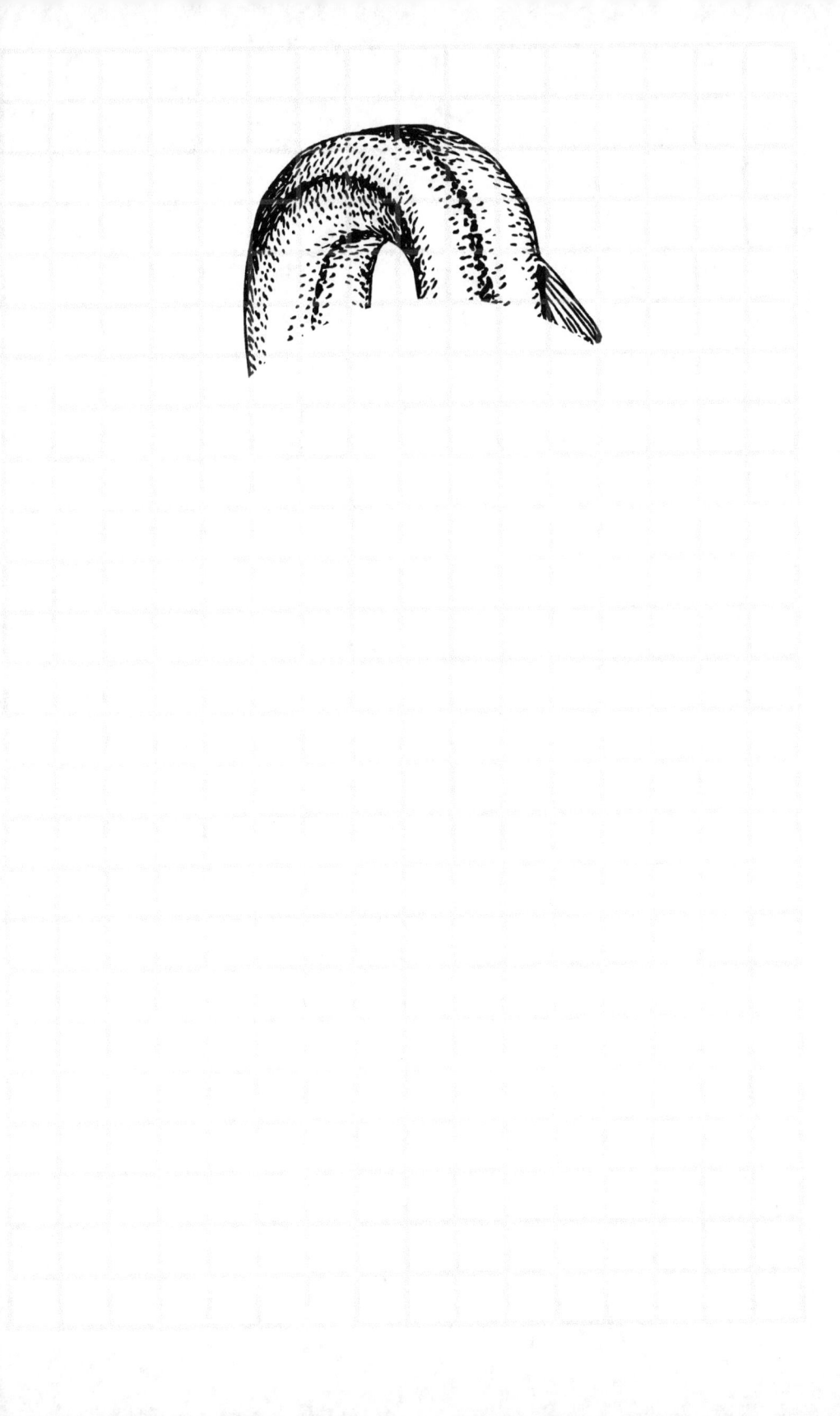

Fish feel pain and stress, just like mammals and birds.

It is estimated that more than 15,000 species of fish have not yet been identified.

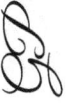

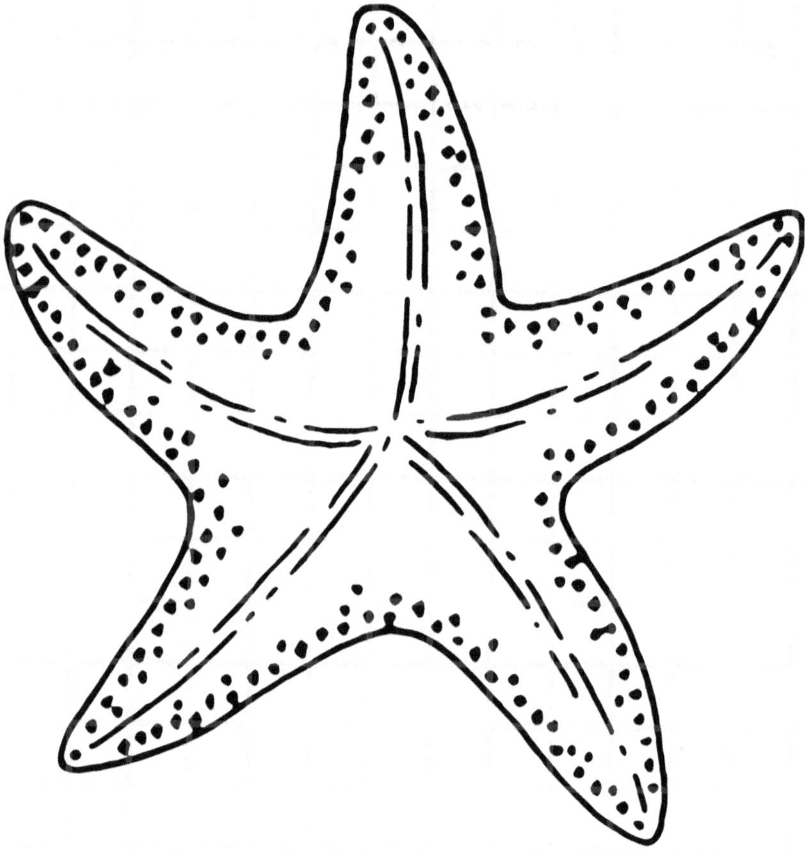

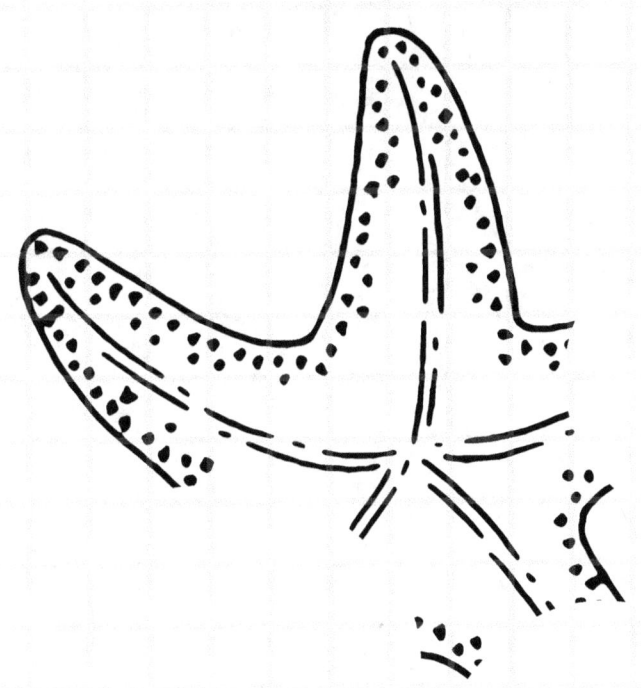

They are very slow, they crawl lazily

Sometimes they are difficult to notice because they hide in crevices and recesses of rocks

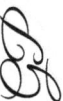

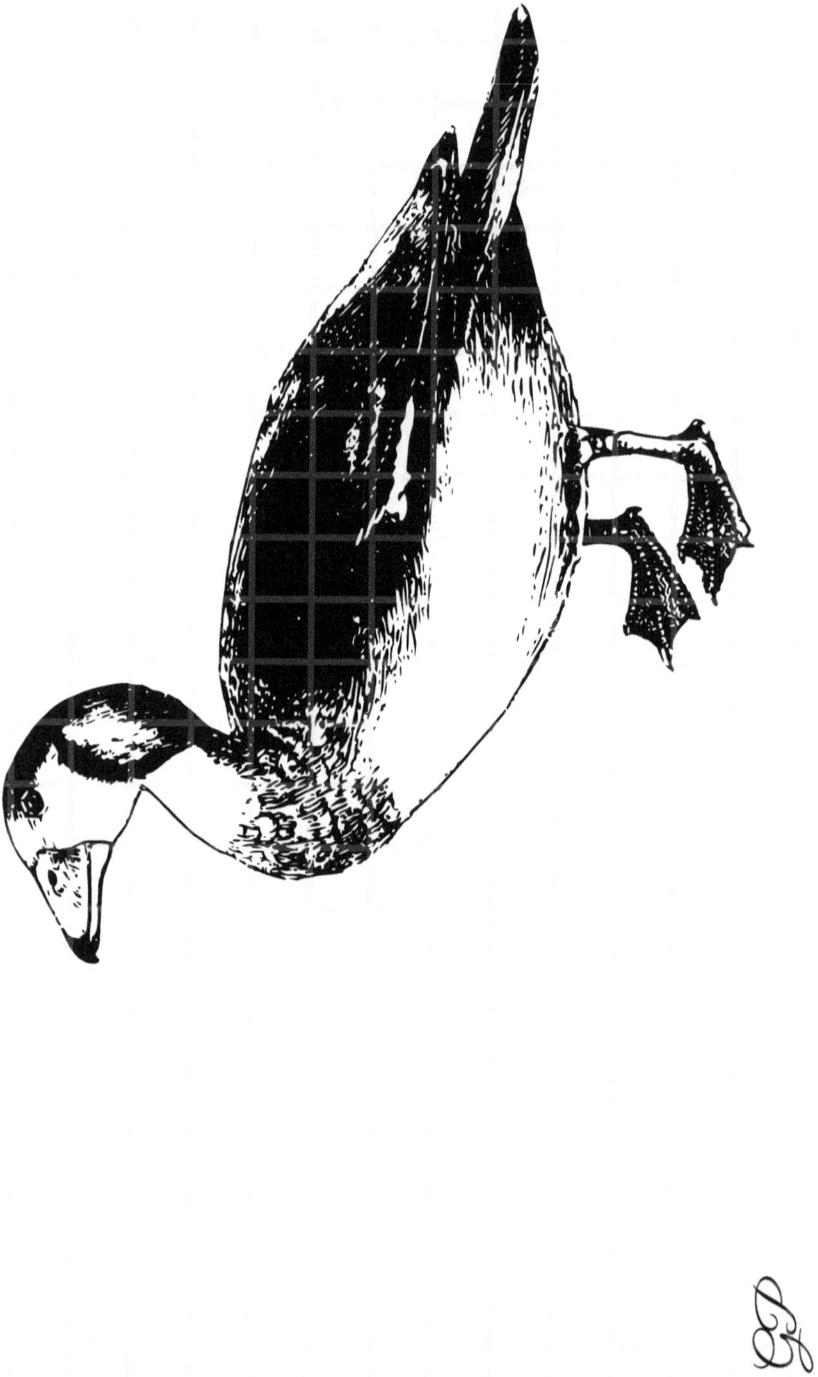

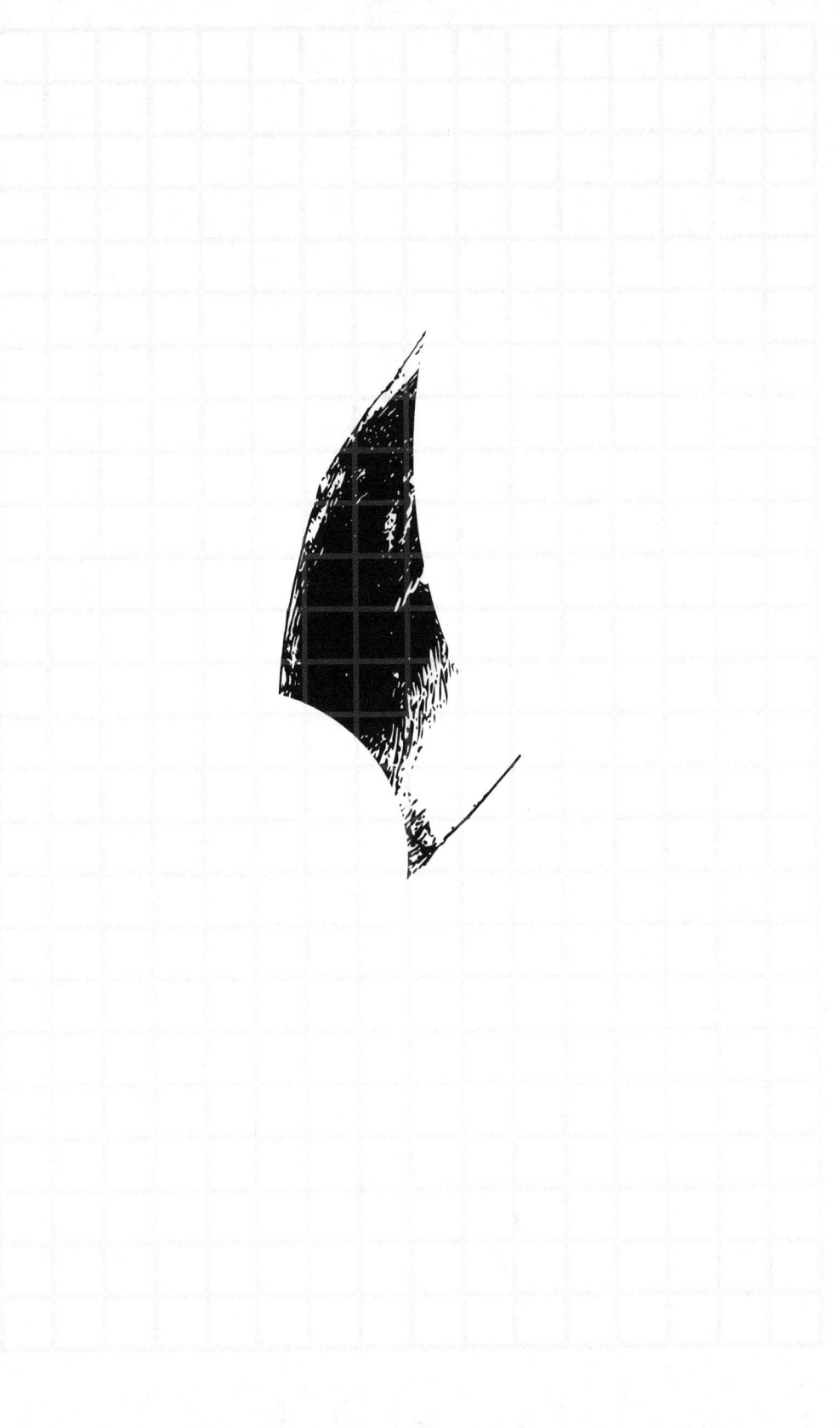

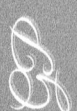

Ducks can fly as high as airplanes.

Ducks can live from 2 to 12 years, depending on the species.

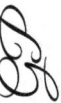

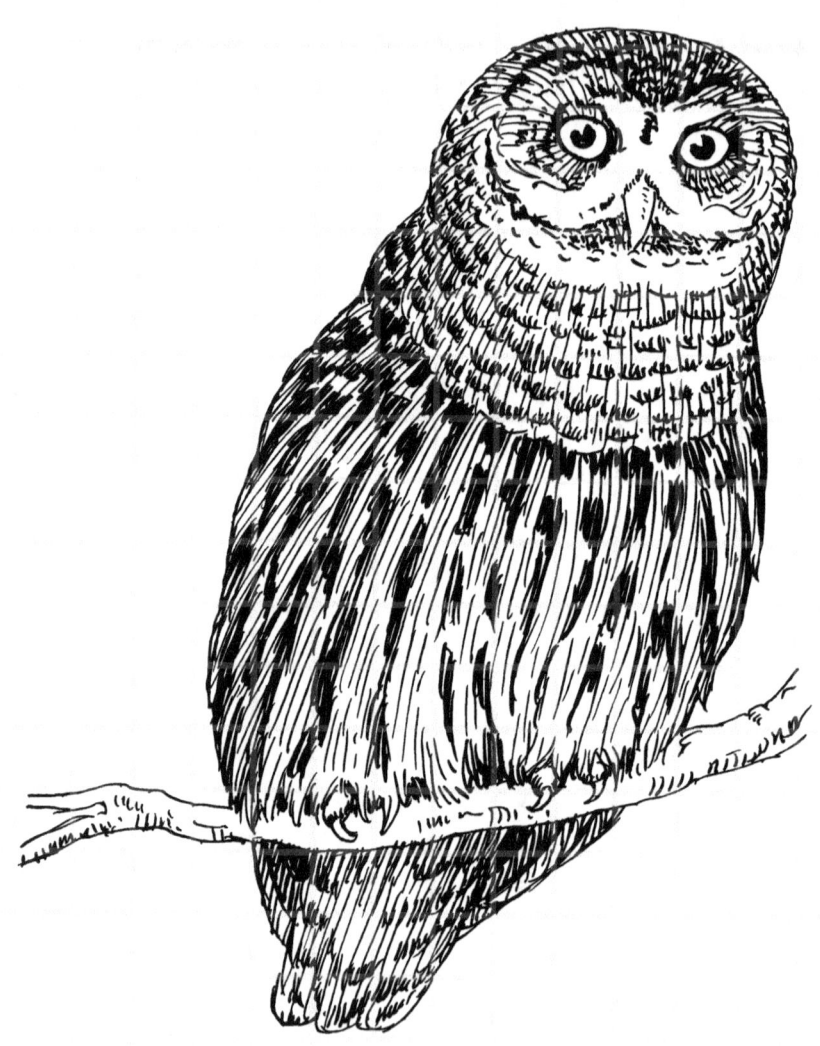

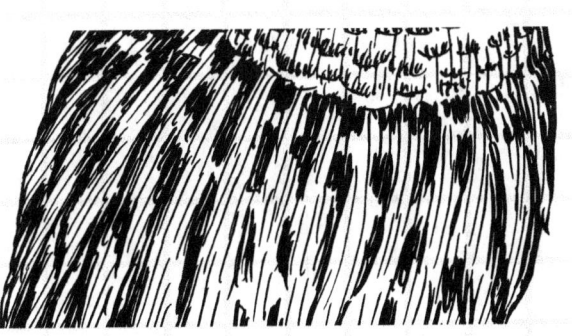

Not all owls are active at night

Sight - night-active owls see perfectly in the dark

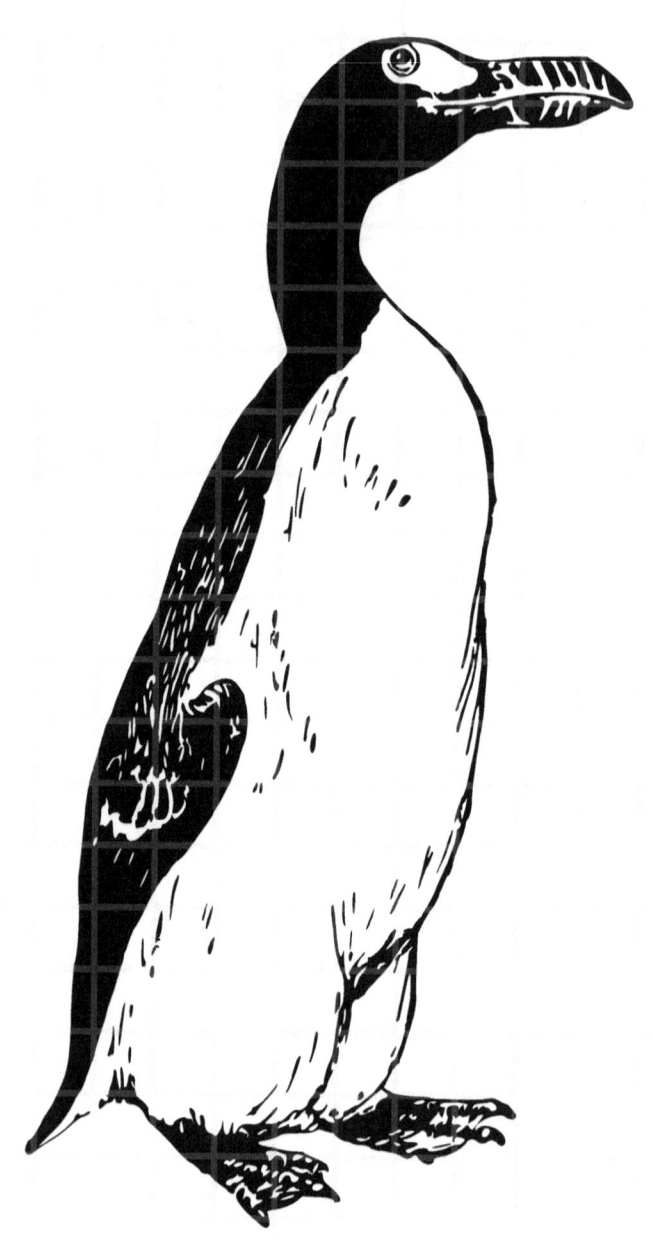

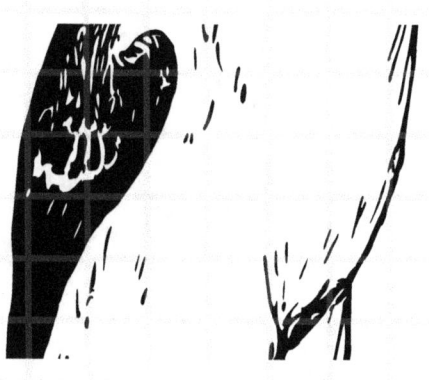

There are 17 species of these flightless birds.

Penguins are the only birds that maintain an upright posture.

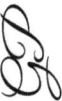

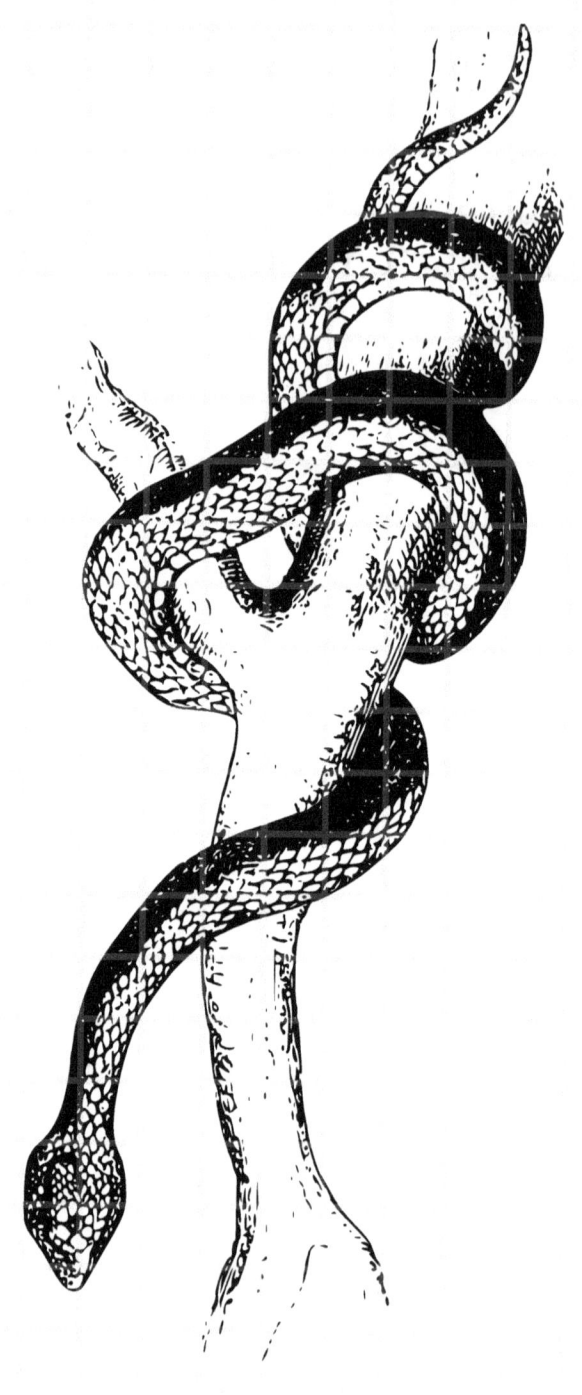

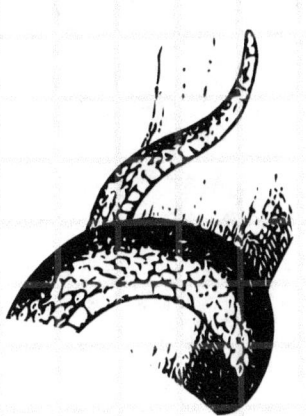

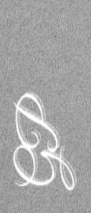

About 20% of all snakes are venomous species.

They swallow their victims whole.

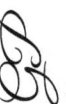

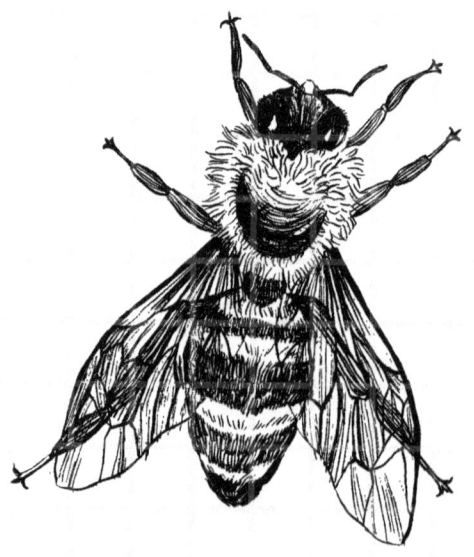

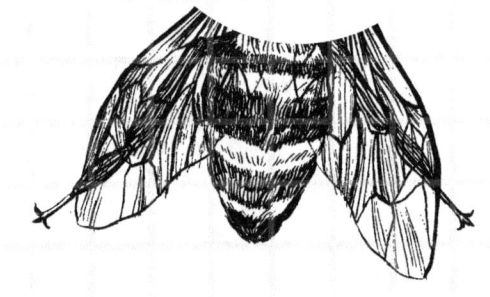

Bees communicate by dancing and making sounds

There are about 20,000 species of bees in the world.

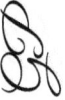

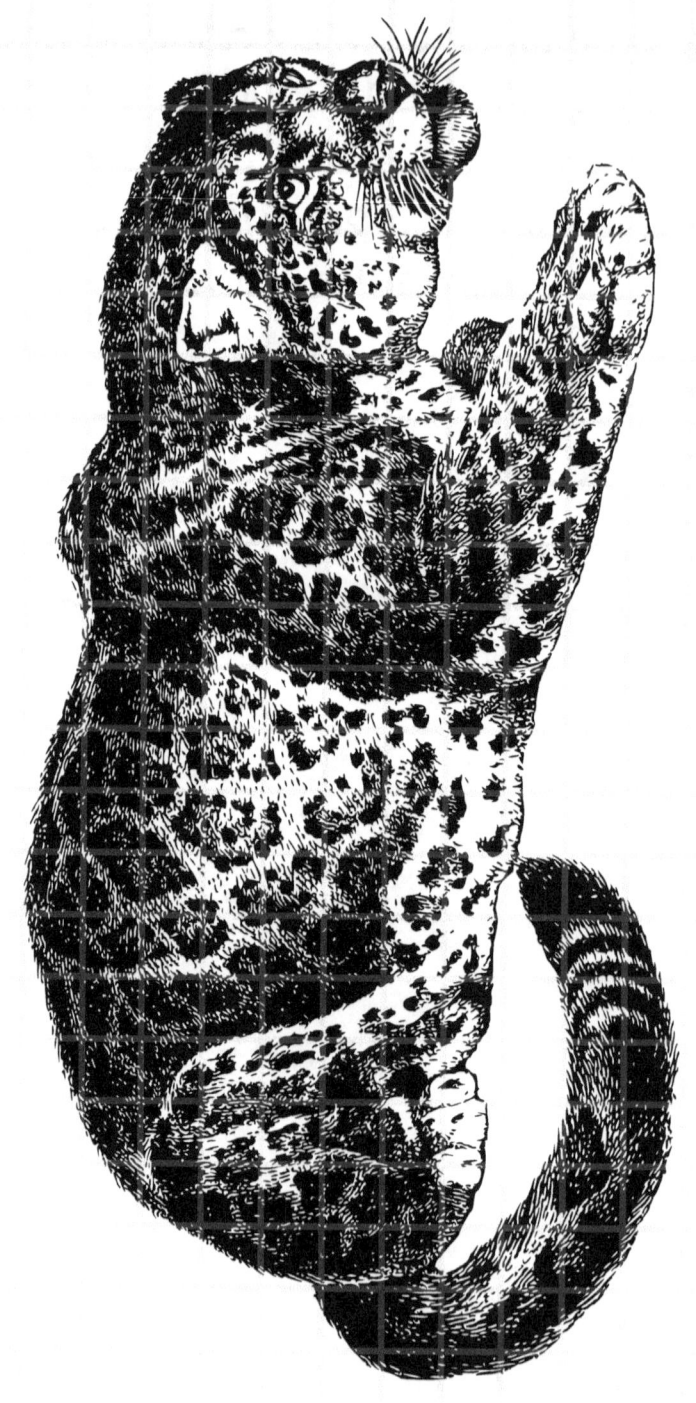

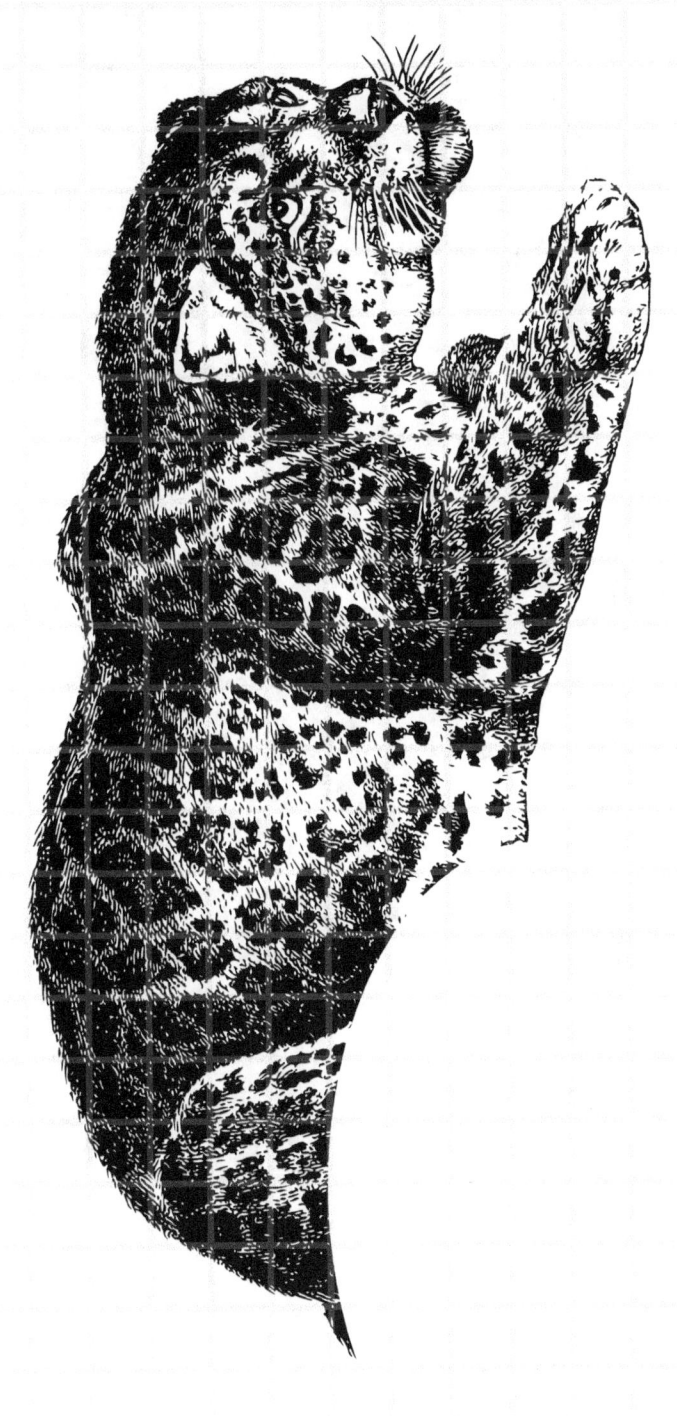

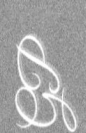

They are one of the few cats that cannot hide their claws

Cheetahs are the fastest land animals in the world

THANKS FOR YOUR PURCHASE AND SUPPORT

LEAVE A COMMENT AND RATING

IF YOU NEED MORE STUFF CHECK AUTHOR:

PAOLA RAZZO

ON AMAZON

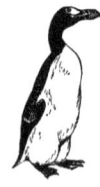

SHARE YOUR DRAWINGS

Comment, rate and share the product so that I can continue to create

FB: Galas Products

Pinterest: https://pl.pinterest.com/GalasProducts

Instagram: Galasproducts

Twitter: @GalasProducts

COPYRIGHT © 2020 BY GALAS DARIUSZ ALL RIGHTS RESERVED

www.ingramcontent.com/pod-product-compliance
Lightning Source LLC
Chambersburg PA
CBHW050245220526
45465CB00002B/560